# IN PRAISE OF MARY

## MARY

Hymns from the first millennium
of the Eastern and Western Churches

 St Paul Publications

Texts selected by Costante Berselli and Giorgio Gharib
Co-ordinated with notes by Costante Berselli

The hymns arranged in this volume
are taken from a larger collection entitled *Lodi alla Madonna*,
edited by C. Berselli and G. Gharib and published in a paperback
edition by Edizioni Paoline in the series "Letture Cristiane delle Origini"

Iconographic research by M. Luisa Badenchini

Translated from the Italian by Phil Jenkins

Acknowledgement is made to the Grail, England, for permission
to reproduce their translation of the Magnificat

## St Paul Publications
Middlegreen, Slough SL3 6BT

Copyright © St Paul Publications 1981

First published May 1981

ISBN 085439 187 8

Printed in Italy by Istituto Grafico Bertello
Borgo San Dalmazzo

*St Paul Publications is an activity of the priests and brothers of the
Society of St Paul who promote the christian message through the
mass media.*

# PREFACE

Turning over the pages of this book the reader, art lover or not, cannot but marvel at the excellent miniatures which are reproduced here.

The miniature, as illustration of the manuscript book, had a remarkable stimulus in the Middle Ages with the renewal of study and the impetus given to culture. The purpose of the miniature, like that later on of engraving, and in our day of photography, was to illustrate and match a text. The scribes of the Benedictine monasteries were the first to apply this to their liturgical books, antiphoners, lectionaries and graduales, illuminating first the capitals and then the whole page of the parchment manuscripts.

When lay students of these monasteries had learnt the art, they started the first studios which developed later into proper schools of miniatures, and from which emerged the masters who are linked to the history of art.

With the circulation of books, still in manuscript form, the situation was reversed and the abbeys became purchasers of the miniaturists' craft, followed in the fourteenth and fifteenth centuries by the rulers of the major and minor dominions that had asserted their authority in the Italian peninsula. These latter had become collectors of codices illuminated with texts of the classics of literature and science kept at the court libraries, as well as of devotional books, again illuminated, for the use of the laity, such as the Office of the Blessed Virgin and the well-known "Book of the Hours", prayer books derived from the Breviary.

It was the epoch in which the illuminated codex became the object of that patronage whereby the mediaeval "lord" saw a reflection of the splendour of his court.

Turning our attention back to admire the miniatures reproduced here, let the reader who turns over the pages of this book make his own the carefully-pursued intent of honouring with the work of art a short collection of praises to Our Lady, inspired expression of the first Christian communities of the East and the West.

Recovered like a lost inheritance, these hymns of praise become the counterpoint to accompany the sense of musical appreciation the artist makes one feel, whenever one intuits the underlying endeavour of his precise, detailed and polychrome work.

From another viewpoint, the hymns of praise so rich in poetic form with charming titles directed to the Virgin but nevertheless full of christological doctrine, merit the posthumous honour of being presented within the frame of artistic miniatures of which they were, substantially, the inspirers.

From the hymns of praise to the miniatures, from painting and sculpture to the marian shrines, the religious sense of the faithful during the stream of time of the Church's history has woven a garland to crown the Virgin Mother of God, mediatrix between Christ and humankind.

C.B.

# Six illuminated codices

The miniatures reproduced here have been taken from six codices kept in the Este Library of Modena and from a codex of the State Archives of Turin.

## GRADUALE (Lat. 1016)

Miniatures of the Bolognese school attributed to the end of the 13th century and to the beginning of the 14th century, with obvious Byzantine influences. Reproduced are: initial S with the Purification of the Virgin; initial A with Madonna and Child; initial D with the birth of the Baptist; initial G with the death of Our Lady; again initial G with Jesus enthroned; initial R with the Annunciation; again initial S with the Virgin and Child; initial L with the Virgin with the Child on her knee; again initial A with Our Lady in a violet cloak, with the Child.

Pages 69 - 77 - 19 - 67 - 27 - 15 - 57 - 63 - 83

## ANTIPHONALE (Lat. 1003)

Miniature of the Bolognese school from the studio of Nicolò di Giacomo (14th century). The reproduction is of the letter H with the crib.

Page 81

## GRADUALE (Lat. 1005)

Miniatures of the Bolognese school attributed to the end of the 13th century and to the beginning of the 14th century. Reproduced are: initial R with the Annunciation; initial O with Our Lady on the way to Bethlehem; initial L with the Holy Family; initial P with Madonna and Child; initial E with the Adoration of the Magi; initial N with the Crucifixion; Double-page picture of the sepulchre of Jesus.

Pages 39 - 75 - 73 - 55 - 45 - 87 - 70, 71

## OFFICE OF THE BLESSED VIRGIN (Lat. 842)

Miniatures of the Lombardy school from the last decade of the 14th century. These full-page miniatures show: the Annunciation; the Birth of Jesus; the Adoration of the Magi; Our Lady enthroned; the Assumption of the Virgin; the Crucified Lord; a Greek gold cross; the Pietà.

Pages  21 - 51 - 33 - 17 - 23 - 59 - 79 - 65

## OFFICE OF THE BLESSED VIRGIN (Lat. 893)

Miniatures from the Franco-Flemish school from the beginning of the 15th century. Here are reproduced, all with frieze and border: the Annunciation; the visit of Our Lady to St Elizabeth; the Virgin and Child; the Message to the shepherds; the Adoration of the Magi; the presentation at the Temple; the flight into Egypt; the Virgin at Prayer; the prophet David; the Crucifixion; Pentecost; the Last Judgement; Madonna and Child.

Pages   41 - 13 - 31 - 35 - 29 - 61 - 43 - 89 - 37 - 47 - 53 - 25 - 49

## LIVRE DE LAUDES ET DEVOTIONS

Miniature of the 15th century. It portrays the Glory of Mary among the Angels and Saints, framed within a splendid surrounding frieze with plant life.

Page 85

# IN PRAISE OF MARY

# My soul glorifies the Lord

y soul glorifies the Lord,
my spirit rejoices in God, my Saviour.
He looks on his servant in her nothingness;
henceforth all ages will call me blessed.
The Almighty works marvels for me.
Holy his name!
His mercy is from age to age
on those who fear him.
He puts forth his arm in strength
and scatters the proud-hearted.
He casts the mighty from their thrones
and raises the lowly.
He fills the starving with good things,
sends the rich away empty.
He protects Israel, his servant,
remembering his mercy,
The mercy promised to our fathers,
for Abraham and his sons for ever.
Praise the Father, the Son and Holy Spirit,
both now and for ever, world without end.

*Luke 1, 46-55*

*The Visit of Our Lady to St Elizabeth*

e came from heaven
took mortal form.
To Gabriel was first revealed
the one most chaste and true;
Thus spoke the archangel
to the maiden:
"Receive, O Virgin,
The Lord in your immaculate womb".
At these words
the Lord gave grace to her
who was to be for ever Virgin.
She, to hear these words,
was filled with wonder and with dread.
In stillness she stood trembling
bewildered, as one lost,
the while her heart did throb
to hear the wondrous news.
Then jumped her heart with joy
to find comfort in those words.
She smiled, with blushing cheek,
delighting in her joy,
heart filled with gentle modesty.
And courage came again
and soared the Word within her womb.
He would in time be flesh
and taking life within the womb,
assume the form of mortal man
and be born a child, a child of virgin birth.
This is a great marvel for humankind.
But nothing is too great
for God the Father, God the Son.

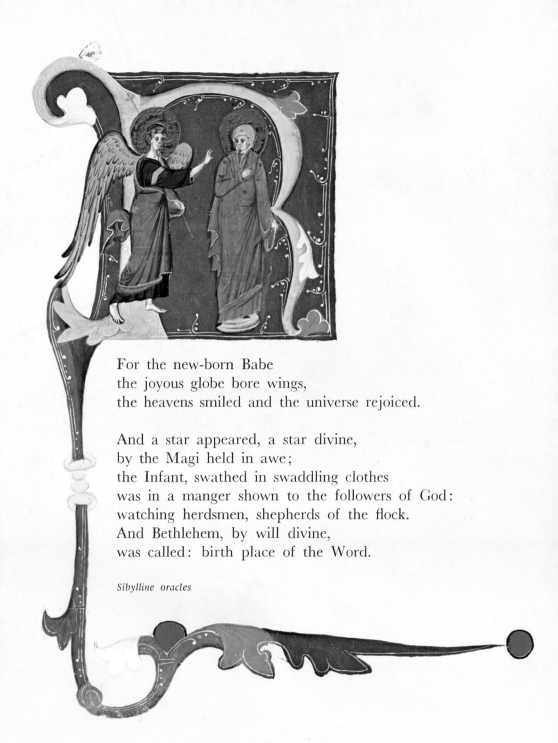

For the new-born Babe
the joyous globe bore wings,
the heavens smiled and the universe rejoiced.

And a star appeared, a star divine,
by the Magi held in awe;
the Infant, swathed in swaddling clothes
was in a manger shown to the followers of God:
watching herdsmen, shepherds of the flock.
And Bethlehem, by will divine,
was called: birth place of the Word.

*Sibylline oracles*

*The Annunciation of the Archangel Gabriel to the Virgin*

In the shadow of your mercy
we shelter, O Mother of God

 n the shadow of your mercy
we shelter, O Mother of God.
Do not ignore our supplications
in our temptation,
but deliver us from danger,
O pure one, blessed one.

*Egyptian papyrus, 3rd century*

*Our Lady enthroned suckling her Child*

It was vital to us
that God should become man

ow can we fittingly exchange
an honour so great
so full of love?
The Only Son of God,
begotten of unutterable divine origin,
taking shape in the womb of the Holy Virgin,
grows into the form of a human being.
He who holds all
and in whom and for whom
all things exist
was born
according to the laws of human nature;
the One at whose voice
angels and archangels tremble,
heaven and earth
and all the elements
of this world dissolve,
the Invisible One,
He who cannot be incapsulated in any human reality,
He whom we cannot see,
feel or touch,
behold him in his crib, in swaddling clothes.
The person who reflects on these things,
unworthy of a God,
will feel the more for being loved
just because they are in contrast
with divine grandeur.

He, by means of whom
man was made,
had no need to become man;
but it was vital to us
that God should become man
and live in us;
that is, by taking on humanity,
he should live in all of us.
His humiliation is our greatness,
his degradation is our honour;
on the one hand, God was born a man
on the other, the antithesis,
we were reborn in God.

*St Hilary of Poitiers*

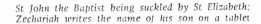

*St John the Baptist being suckled by St Elizabeth;*
*Zechariah writes the name of his son on a tablet*

## Hail, full of grace,
## the Lord is with you

 ail, Virgin Mother of God,
full of grace,
the Lord is with you.
Blessed are you among women
and blessed is the fruit of your womb,
for you have begotten
the Saviour of our souls.

*Ostrakon, 5th century*

20

*The Annunciation of the angel to Mary. The Eternal Father gives
his blessing and from the dove descend golden rays*

# O Virgin,
## your glory transcends all created things

O Virgin, your glory transcends all created things.
What, in effect, compares to your nobility,
O Mother of God the Word?
To what in all creation will I compare you?
Angels of God and archangels are sublime,
but how much you transcend them, O Mary!
Angels and archangels in trembling serve him
who lives within your womb,
and venture not to speak;
you, on the contrary, speak freely with him!
We say that cherubs are sublime,
but you are more sublime than they:
cherubs support the throne of God,
you, on the contrary, support God within your arms.
Seraphs are close to God,
but you are closer than they:
Seraphs hide their faces with their wings
unable to look at the perfect glory,
you, on the contrary, not only contemplate his face,
but caress him
and suckle his holy mouth.

*Athanasius of Alexandria*

*The Assumption of the Virgin, borne by cherubims and
received by Jesus with open arms*

You have received within you the One
that nothing in the world could him contain

 he angel comes to Mary, and entering, says:
Hail, full of grace!
In an instant he exalts the maiden and treats
her as a woman,
for she has become the mother of the Lord.

Hail, full of grace!
Your ancestress, Eve, transgressing,
was condemned to bear her sons in pain.
You, on the contrary, he fills with joy.
She gave birth to Cain
and with him, envy and death.
You, on the contrary, beget a son
who is for all the source of life incorruptible.

Hail, therefore and rejoice.
Hail, the serpent's head is crushed.
Hail, full of grace!
For calamity is at an end,
corruption is dissolved,
all sadness now has ceased,
joy has flourished,
the glad tidings of the prophets
have come to pass.
The Holy Spirit foretold,
speaking through Isaiah's mouth:
Behold, a virgin shall conceive
and bear a son (Is 7:14).
You are this virgin.

The Last Judgement: Christ in judgement seated on a rainbow
showing the wounds of his Passion

Hail, then, full of grace!
You are the delight of him who has created you . . .
You are the delight of those who rejoice in the beauty of
    the soul;
you have found a spouse who protects your virginity
leaving it undefiled;
a spouse who, out of such great love,
willed to become your son.

The Lord is with you!
He is in you and in every place,
he is with you and of you . . .
The Son in the bosom of his Father,
the Only Begotten Son in your womb,
the Lord, in the way known alone to him,
all in everyone
and all in you!

Blessed are you among women!
For you have been placed above all virgins,
for you have been found worthy
to give shelter to the Lord,
for you have received within you the One who is so great
that nothing in the world could him contain,
you have received him who fills all with himself,
for you have become the place
in which has come to pass salvation,
for you have been the vehicle that has ushered in
the King to life,
for you have appeared as a treasure, a spiritual pearl.
Blessed are you among women!

*Gregory of Nyssa*

*Jesus, enthroned, offers the crown to one of the eleven thousand virgins and martyrs*

## Hail, Mother of Christ,
## Son of the Living God

 ail, song of cherubs
　　　and angels' praises.
Hail, peace and joy
　　　of the human race.
Hail, garden of delight,
　　hail, O fuel of life.
Hail, bulwark of the faithful
　　and port of the shipwrecked.
Hail, reminder of Adam,
　　hail, ransom of Eve.
Hail, fount of grace
　　and immortality.
Hail, temple most holy,
　　hail, throne of the Lord.
Hail, O chaste one, who have crushed
　　the serpent's head
　　hurling him into the abyss.
Hail, refuge of the afflicted,
　　hail, ransom of the curse.
Hail, O Mother of Christ,
　　Son of the Living God,
　　to whom shall be glory, honour,
　　adoration and praise
　　both now and for ever and everywhere.
And for ever, Amen.

*Ephraem Syrus*

28

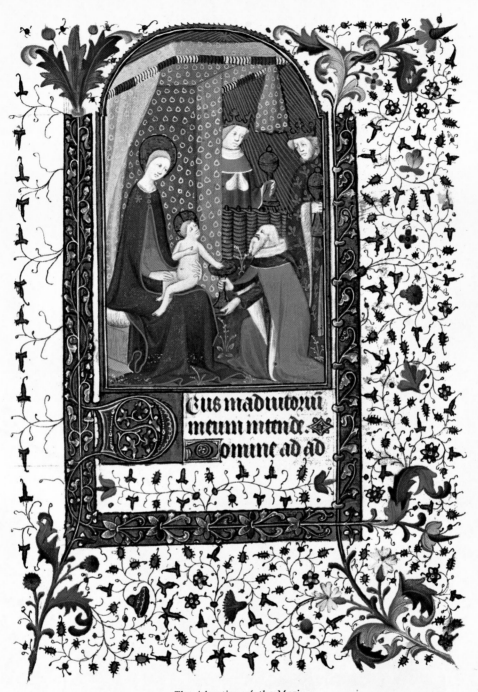

*The Adoration of the Magi*

Wondrously you descended
into the pure womb of the Virgin Mary

 true Light, our Lord God,
who from the depths of your heart
have voiced the saving Word,
we pray to you:
as wondrously you descended
into the pure womb of the Virgin Mary,
grant us, your servants,
to await with joy
the glorious nativity.

*The Scroll of Ravenna*

*The Virgin adores the Child Jesus*

You have made a holy dwelling in the flesh

 God, who in the Virgin's womb
with wondrous art,
have made
a holy dwelling in the flesh:
Come, you righteous one,
come swiftly
and, according to the ancient promise,
ransom man from his plight.
To you let there rise up the praise
worthy of so great a love
and to us be given eternal salvation.

*The Scroll of Ravenna*

*The adoration of the Kings who remove their crowns*
*and kneel to kiss the feet of the Babe*

The womb that knew no human blemish
was shelter for the Lord

**t** is truly suitable and wise,
just and beneficial
to give thanks to you, almighty and eternal God,
that Jesus Christ, our Lord,
has come upon the earth.
Through love, from heaven he descended,
emerged from the sanctuary of the Virgin's body.
Scarce he appeared as Saviour of humankind
than did the angels sing "glory in the highest heavens"
and they exulted
for earth had received the King of ages.
Mary, the blessed one, became the precious temple
to keep watch o'er the Lord of lords.
To take away our sins
she begot Life sublime;
and Life vanquished bitter death.
The womb that knew no human blemish
was worthy shelter for the Lord.
Born into the world is he
who lived in heaven for ever
and still in heaven lives.

*Gallican Liturgy*

*The Message to the shepherds: the angel carries the announcement written on a scroll*

## Holy Mary, who sprang from our world and from our lineage

et the peoples honour you, O God,
let all the peoples honour you".
We said it once
and were not heard;
we repeat it, so that you may acclaim it . . .
Why do we insist again?
This earth has given its fruit,
The earth: Holy Mary
who sprang from our world
and from our lineage . . . .
Ths earth has given its fruit,
and finds in the Son
what was lost in Eden.
"The earth has given its fruit".
First, it gave the flower . . .
The flower became a fruit
for us to eat,
and be nourished by it . . .
The son is born of the Virgin,
the Lord of the maiden,
God of humankind,
The Son of the Mother,
the fruit of the earth.

*Jerome*

*King David at prayer in the presence of his God*

## Hail, seat of the infinite God, gateway of majestic mystery

ail, you who carried in your womb
  the guide for all who stray;
Hail, you who have borne
  the deliverer of servants;
Hail, appeaser of the just judge;
  Hail, pardon for those who have repented;
Hail, refuge for those who despair;
  Hail, love which surpasses all desire;
Hail, chaste spouse!
  Wondering at the birth unearthly
  we become strangers to the world
  turning our thoughts to heaven . . .
. . . the Most High
as a poor man appeared upon the earth,
wishing to raise on high
all those who proclaim:
Alleluia! . . .

The Son was born of the Virgin,
and, in welcoming her God,
to her ears came the words:
Hail, seat of the infinite God,
  Hail, gateway of majestic mystery . . .

The Creator of all things,
wanting to save the world,
of his own will came into the world.
He, God, although our Shepherd,
for us, appeared among us as a man.
Having thus called us all together,
He, God, listens:
Alleluia!

You are the protector of virgins, O Virgin Mother of God,
and of all those who turn to you.
The Creator of heaven and of earth
made you thus immaculate,
to dwell within your womb
and to teach all to sing to you:
Hail, pillar of virginity,
    Hail, gateway of salvation,
Hail, initiator of new issue,
    Hail, manifestation of the divine goodness,
Hail, you who have given new life
    to all who were begotten in sin . . .

*The Annunciation: the angel blesses
the Virgin who carries a scroll of
Holy Scripture in her hand*

Fail must every hymn
that attempts to equate
your infinite mercy, O God.
If hymns we were to sing to you,
as many as grains of sand, O King,
never could we match the worth
that you have given us,
for we proclaim:
Alleluia!

*Akathistos Hymn*

Blessed are we who have you
as our defence

 irgin Mother of God
we, the peoples of all nations,
proclaim you blessed;
He, who surpasses all things,
Christ, our God, in you has deigned to dwell.
Blessed are we,
who have you as our defence,
for you intercede night and day for us . . .
And so we hymn our praise to you, proclaiming:
Hail, full of grace, the Lord is with you!

*Anonymous Hymn, 5th-6th century*

*The Virgin, kneeling in a chapel receives the angel's message*

# What shall I call you, full of grace?

hat shall I call you, full of grace?
I shall call you Heaven: for you have caused
the Sun of justice to rise.
Paradise: for in you
has bloomed the flower of immortality.
Virgin: for you have remained inviolate.
Chaste Mother: for you have carried in your arms
a Son, the God of all.
Pray to him to save our souls.

*Anonymous Hymn, 5th-6th century*

*The flight into Egypt: St Joseph leads the donkey which carries the Virgin and Child*

## The prayer of a mother can do much to secure the goodwill of the Master

O Virgin Mother of God,
plead with him who is born of you
since we, by reason of our sins,
have no trust in ourselves.
The prayer of a mother can do much
to secure the goodwill of the Master.
He indeed, is merciful
and can deliver us,
he, incarnate, who accepted
to suffer for us.

*Anonymous Hymn, 5th-6th century*

*The Magi adore the Child in the arms of Our Lady*

**A thousand times glorified are you,**
**O Virgin Mother of God!**

 thousand times glorified are you,
O Virgin Mother of God!
We hymn our praise to you
for by the cross of your Son
hell has been overthrown
and death humiliated;
we, who were dead, have been revived
and made worthy of life;
we have gained paradise,
our principal reward.
Therefore, we glorify you, O Christ our God.
the almighty and merciful One.

*Anonymous Hymn, 5th-6th century*

*The Crucifixion of Jesus: Our Lady and St John stand at the foot of the Cross*

## Hail, O countenance illuminated by the light of God from which such beauty flows

 et us be guided by the words of Gabriel,
citizen of heaven, and say:
Hail, full of grace, the Lord is with you!
We say again with him:
Hail, O our such longed-for joy!
Hail, O rapture of the Church!
Hail, O name so full of fragrance!
Hail, O countenance illuminated by the light of God
from which such beauty flows!
Hail, O memorial full of reverence!
Hail, O spiritual and salutary fleece!
Hail, O bright mother of the dawning light!
Hail, O stainless mother of saintliness!
Hail, O gushing fount of living water!
Hail, new mother
moulder of the new-born One!
Hail, O inexplicable and mystery-filled mother! . . .
Hail, O alabaster vase
of holy unction!
Hail, you who give honour to virginity!
Hail, O humble space, which welcomed to itself
Him whom the world cannot contain!

*Theodore of Ancyra*

*The Madonna and Child with two angelic musicians beside her*

# Believe in the salvation which comes from my womb

Who are you that with such faith have conceived
and soon is to become a mother?
The One who created you will be born in you.
Whence came to you such great goodness?
You are virgin, you are holy . . .
Much it is you have merited,
or better, much it is you have received!
He who created you has become incarnate in you:
the Word of God,
through whom the heavens, earth
and all things were made;
The Word, not ceasing to be God,
assumes in you the nature of man,
becomes man . . .
When he was conceived, you were a virgin;
a virgin still, when he was born.
It seems an indiscretion
that I question thus the Virgin
and so disturb her reserve.
But the Virgin, blushing yet, to me replies:
"You ask whence came to me such goodness? . . .
Listen to the angel's greeting
and believe in the salvation which comes from my womb.
Believe in him in whom I have believed".

*Augustine*

*The Birth of Jesus: Our Lady, St Joseph and St Anne kneeling, adore the Holy Child*

You are the only woman, unique and beyond compare,
who was pleasing to Christ

A s much light upon the earth,
as there is grace in all the heavens!
What splendour
when Christ came forth from Mary's womb
such glory had never been seen!
He was like a bridegroom
who comes exulting from his nuptial bed of glory,
handsome with an attractive beauty,
not ordinary like that of man;
radiant is his figure
and on his lips
is seen a gentle grace . . .

Hail, Holy Mother,
who has given birth to the King;
He who governs heaven and earth
in time
and whose divinity and whose dominion,
which do for ever all embrace,
are without end.
Your blessed womb has given you the joy
of motherhood and the honour of virginity;
you are like one who has no equal
among women, before or after you.
You are the only woman, unique and beyond compare,
who was pleasing to Christ.

*Sedulius*

*Pentecost: The Holy Spirit descends in the form of a dove on
Our Lady and the Apostles assembled in the Cenacle*

# The Word of God became flesh

urn to us, you who lead Israel,
you who are seated above the Cherubims;
you who appeared in the presence of Ephraim,
revive your power and come!

Come swiftly, Redeemer of humankind.
Manifest the One who is born of the Virgin.
Let all ages admire him!
Such a birth becomes God.

Through a mystical breath of the Spirit,
not from human seed,
the Word of God became flesh.
The fruit of the womb ripened.

The womb of the Virgin enlarges
but the cloister of modesty remains intact.
The standards of the virtues glitter.
Christ dwells within his temple.

Let him come forth from the chaste and regal womb,
as from his nuptial bed,
the Most High God-man
to briskly run his path.

He came from the Father,
returned to the Father,
descended into hell,
ascended to the throne of God.

You who are equal to the eternal Father,
clothed yourself in our flesh
to strengthen with unfailing vigour
the feebleness of our body.

Resplendent is your manger;
the night irradiates its light;
let no shadow darken it
but always shine with the light of faith.

*Ambrosian Hymn*

*Our Lady enthroned, with the Babe on her knee*

# From you is born the source of your being

irgin,
it was not nature but grace that made you mother:
love willed that you should become mother . . .
With your conceiving, with your giving birth
modesty has increased,
chastity, integrity and virginity
have been strengthened . . .

Virgin,
if all remained untouched,
what have you yielded?
If a virgin, how are you a mother?

Virgin,
he, thanks to whom
everything that is in you has increased,
nothing in you has diminished.

Virgin,
your Creator was in you conceived;
from you is born the source of your being;
he who brought light to the world,
is brought forth from you in the world.

*Peter Chrysologus*

*Our Lady with the Child on her lap*

## Pray to God for us that peace may be strengthened and love increased

 irgin,
give us not only food for the body,
but also the bread of angels
come down into your virginal womb.
Make us fear the Son of God . . .
for he who fears God will keep his commandments
and purify his senses
so as to gaze on the splendour of divine light.
After we have been granted
purification of the senses
there will follow enlightenment
of the heart.
Hear us then, O Virgin benign,
and receive our prayers.
O Virgin . . . pray to God for us
that he will grant us perseverance,
and the strength to endure,
that peace may be strengthened
and love increased;
so that when the day comes
of sorrow and misery,
of calamity and sadness,
you will deign to present us
to your only Son,
who alone is God . . .
Amen.

*Eleutherius of Tournai*

58

*The Crucified Lord: at either side Our Lady and St John,*
*Mary Magdalene kneeling at the foot of the Cross*

## You have gathered the fruit
## of life and of immortality

ail, O most holy Mother
of God our Redeemer
who through you came to live with us
and we with him . . .

Hail, O revered and immaculate Mother of God!
He who from the highest heaven,
without leaving heaven,
came into your womb as into his own home,
he the same Christ the Lord, made you worthy of passing
from this worldly place to the heavenly home,
which he gave, through you, to the saints who him awaited.

Hail, Mary, splendid spiritual paradise!
You have gathered, through the power of the Holy Spirit,
the fruit of life and immortality:
the One who was begotten of the Father, Christ our Lord.
We, partakers of his life through true belief,
in him have been given life.
He built for you, in paradise, a tabernacle,
where you dwell with your glorified body;
through you, for us too, the door is opened.

Hail, O most adorned and shining refuge!
You have been made the Mother of God.
The human race, shipwrecked on the sea of life,
in you is saved;
through you it has obtained the gifts of life
from the One who honoured you in time
and glorifies you for ever and ever.

*Modestus of Jerusalem*

*The presentation of Jesus in the Temple*

# Hail, Mother of celestial joy

ail, mother of celestial joy
Hail, you who nourish in us a joy sublime,
Hail, seat of redeeming joy,
Hail, you who offer us perennial joy,
Hail, O mystical abode of ineffable joy,
Hail, O most worthy place of indescribable joy.

Hail, O blessed spring of infinite joy,
Hail, O divine treasure of endless joy,
Hail, O shady tree of life-giving joy,
Hail, O Mother of God, unwedded bride,
Hail, O Virgin, unblemished after giving birth,
Hail, wondrous vision,
far above any other marvel.

Who could describe your splendour?
Who could tell of your mystery?
Who could know how to proclaim your grandeur?
You have embellished human nature,
you have surpassed the angelic legions . . .
you have surpassed all creatures . . .
we acclaim you: Hail, full of grace!

*Sophronius of Jerusalem*

*Front view of the Virgin seated on a stool, holding the Child on her knee*

**You gave your consent in faith
you begot your Son in the flesh**

O holy Mother of God
who, receiving the angel's message,
conceived the Word,
you gave your consent in faith,
you begot your Son in the flesh,
deeply disturbed by the divine presence,
but trustful in the help of grace:
receive your people's requests, you who can
and fully grant the prayers of each one,
so that, welcoming into your maternal womb
all those who, exiles on the journey of life,
take refuge in you with certain hope,
you may present them, saved,
to the Lord Jesus Christ, your Son.

*Visigothic Book of Prayer*

*Christ rises from the tomb: behind him the Cross and emblems of the Passion*

# You came to us through the Virgin

ou came to us through the Virgin
without violating the gate of her virginity,
neither entering into, nor coming forth from her.
O Lord who can do all things
we implore you with all our strength:
you who granted your Mother
to be both virgin and mother,
through her prayers,
bestow on your catholic Church
an incorruptible faith and fertile charity;
thus will your Church be able to give birth to
a people of believers
and, freed from all guilt,
she may reach you without spot or wrinkle.

*Visigothic Book of Prayer*

*The death of Our Lady witnessed by the Apostles: Christ holds the soul of the Virgin*

## You have become a daughter of your Son, handmaiden of your child

Listen, daughter, and behold:
you have become a daughter of your Son,
handmaiden of your child,
mother of your creator,
bearer of the most high Redeemer.
The King has fallen in love
with the splendour of your beauty
and has deigned to prepare for himself,
a most pure dwelling
in his world.
Obtain for us, therefore, from him
who, taken by longing for you,
made you his mother,
to pour into us the wondrous sweetness
of desire for him,
so that we remain dedicated to his service
in this life,
and our journey o'er,
without chaos we arrive
with him who was born of you.

*Visigothic Book of Prayer*

*The Purification of the Virgin. Mary, followed by St Joseph,
presents Jesus to Simeon*

Welcome the people who have recourse to you

O Maiden and most holy Mother of the Word . . .
from the depths of your compassion
welcome the people who have recourse to you.
Nourish, with the outflow of your loving kindness,
the flock which the son born of you
with his blood redeemed.

*The sepulchre of Jesus watched over by soldiers with the lamenting Mary and weeping women*

Offer your bosom to all who are created,
you who nourished the creator of all.
As a reward of service to you
extol all who come to pay their homage.
And we who are happy to serve you
will always be protected
by your mediation.

*Visigothic Book of Prayer*

# Hail, O torrent of compassion

ail, O torrent of compassion,
river of peace and of grace,
splendour of purity, dew of the valleys:
Mother of God and mother of forgiveness.
Hail, only salvation of your children,
solemn throne of majesty,
place of shelter, temple of Christ,
the way to life, lily of chastity.
Hail, spouse of Christ,
flower of lovable grace,
humble maidservant.
Most beautiful and worthy of reverence,
no other woman was or can be like you.
We acclaim you: revered one,
your spirit is pure, and simple your heart,
chaste is your body.
You are indulgent and merciful,
dear to God, beloved above all.
The person who savours you, ardently desires you still,
still thirsts for your holy sweetness,
and always unfulfilled, confines his longing
to loving you and praising you.

*Ildefonsus of Toledo*

*The Holy Family: the Virgin resting on a bed at the foot of which is seated*
*St Joseph. Above, lies the Child*

## Guide for my journey,
## support for my feebleness

my sole comfort,
divine dew, refreshment for my thirst,
rain that comes down from God on the dryness
of my heart,
shining lantern in the darkness of my soul,
guide for my journey,
support for my feebleness,
shelter for my nakedness,
wealth for my extreme poverty,
balm for my incurable wounds,
end of my tears and of my lamentations,
deliverer from all misfortune,
comfort for my sorrows,
deliverer from my slavery,
hope of my salvation . . .

This you are, O my Lady;
this you are, O my refuge,
my life and my help,
my protector and my glory,
my hope and my strength.

Grant that I may enjoy the indescribable
and incomprehensible gifts of your Son
in our heavenly home.
You possess, in effect, I am aware,
a might equal to your will,
for you are the Mother of the Most High;
so thus do I dare and confide.
O most pure Queen
may I not be deceived in my expectations.

*Germanus of Constantinople*

*Our Lady seated on an ass, going to Bethlehem*
*with St Joseph, led by a youth*

 Virgin, from you
as from an unhewn mount,
Christ was carved, the cornerstone
which has interlinked the divided peoples.
For this we rejoice
and glorify you, O Theotokos!

Come, let us remember with pure heart
and chastened soul, the Daughter of the King,
the splendour of the Church,
more resplendent than gold,
and let us glorify her!

Hail! and rejoice, O Spouse of the great King,
you who splendidly reflect
the beauty of your spouse,
and exclaim with your people:
O Giver of life,
we glorify you!

O Saviour, give your heavenly aid
to your Church;
She acknowledges you, she glorifies you,
she recognises no other God
or deliverer except you,
who laid down your life for her.

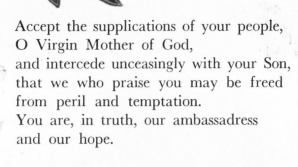

Accept the supplications of your people,
O Virgin Mother of God,
and intercede unceasingly with your Son,
that we who praise you may be freed
from peril and temptation.
You are, in truth, our ambassadress
and our hope.

*Andrew of Crete*

*Our Lady seated with the Child on her knee*

**Of your womb he has made a throne
greater than the heavens**

n you rejoices, O full of grace,
all creation,
the company of angels
and all humankind.
O holy temple and spiritual paradise,
O pride of virgins.
Thanks to you, God took flesh
becoming a child,
he, our God, foremost of all ages.
Of your womb he has made, in truth, a throne
and formed it greater than the heavens.
In you, O full of grace,
all creation rejoices.
Glory to you.

*John of Damascus*

*Greek cross in gold on rose-coloured background, ornamented with gold*

## O Mary, who nurtured in your womb the fruit of oblation

O Mary, immensity of heaven,
foundation of the earth,
depth of the seas, light of the sun,
beauty of the moon,
splendour of the stars in the heavens . . .
Your womb bore God,
before whose majesty man stands in awe.
Your lap held the glowing coal.
Your knees supported the lion,
whose majesty is fearful.
Your hands touched
the One who is untouchable
and the fire of the divinity which is in him.
Your fingers resemble the glowing tongs
with which the prophet received the coals
of the heavenly oblation.
You are the basket for this bread of ardent flame
and the chalice for this wine.
O Mary, who nurtured in your womb
the fruit of oblation . . .
we pray to you with perseverance
to guard us from the adversity which ensnares us
and as the measure of water
cannot be parted from the wine,
so let us not be separated from you and your Son,
the Lamb of salvation.

*Ethiopic Anaphora*

*Our Lady and St Joseph adoring the Babe:
outside the hut two shepherds with their flock*

Port of all who steer
through the misfortunes of life

alm, O maiden most pure,
the wild storm of my soul,
for you alone showed yourself on earth to be
the port of all who set a course
through the perils of life.
You who gave birth to the Light,
brighten, O Pure Lady, the eyes of my heart.
You were given to us on earth
as protection, bulwark and boast.
You were given to us as a tower
and sure salvation, O maiden.
For this we no longer fear adversary,
we who devoutly glorify you.

*Joseph the Studite*

*Our Lady holds her Child on her knee and talks to him*

# Direct with assurance our whole life

o us, therefore, your useless servants,
who with fear and longing dare to exalt you
and address our petitions to you, great Lady,
grant the remission of sins
and triumph over our enemies, visible and invisible;
grant healing to the sick,
grant to the healthy
a sense of gratitude and love for God,
to those who are divided grant unity,
to those who live in harmony with others
grant protection and stability,
to the disheartened and to the afflicted
grant pleasing consolation.
To those who are reluctant to follow the light of reason
send the light of divine grace.
Be a companion to those who journey,
steer with the one who is on the sea,
a support for him who falls,
a buttress for him who stands firm,
prosperity for him who has made good,
help for him who is in need.
Direct with assurance our whole life,
make us worthy of the splendour of the saints above
for, while we raise our hymns of praise
to you, our protectress,
we, together with them, render glory to your Son and God,
with the everlasting Father
and the Holy Spirit, the giver of life,
both now and always, for ever and ever.
Amen!

*Peter of Argus*

Dmine lab mea apri
es.
t os meum annun
nabit laudem tuam.

*Our Lady and Child in the glory of the Angels and Saints*

## Promptly you attend to the voice of those who pray to you

oly Mary, succour the wretched,
help the disheartened,
put new heart into the feeble.
Pray for the people,
intervene for the clergy,
intercede for all holy women.
May all those who honour your memory
experience your generous help.
Promptly you attend to the voice of those who pray to you
and satisfy the desire of each one.
Let your undertaking be diligent intercession
for the people of God.
For you have merited, O blessed one,
to bear the ransom of the world,
he who lives and reigns
for ever and ever.

*Fulbert of Chartres*

*The Crucifixion: Our Lady and St John beside the Cross*

# Hail, O star of the sea, glorious Mother of God

ail, O star of the sea,
glorious Mother of God;
O Holy Virgin, Mary,
O wide-open gate of heaven!

The angel sent by heaven
carries a message from God.
You welcome him:
changes then the destiny of Eve
and peace smiles on the world.

Break the chains of all oppression,
proffer your light to those who cannot see,
drive evil from every person,
beg for each one all that is good.

Let everyone experience that you are our Mother.
Present our prayers to Christ
and may he, who became your Son,
with tender mercy receive them.

Virgin sublime, sweet and beloved,
free us from our guilt,
make us humble and pure.
Give us tranquil days,
keep watch over our path
until that day we shall meet your Son,
joyfully in heaven.

*Popular Hymn, 9th century*

*The Coronation of the Virgin: God the Father raises his right hand in blessing,*
*and holds in his left hand the golden globe*

## The mystery hidden from the beginning comes to light today

he mystery hidden from the beginning
comes to light today and the Son of God
becomes the Son of man, so that,
assuming the limits of humanity
he could raise me above human nature.
Adam was deceived;
he could not become God as he imagined;
instead God becomes man to deify Adam.
Let creation rejoice, the earth dance,
for an archangel did appear
to the Virgin revered,
the bearer of joy — "Rejoice" —
where sorrow held sway.
Glory to you, our God, who for love became man!

*Theophanus the "marked one"*

# The earth covered itself with blessings and beauty

ome, O festive angels,
let us prepare ourselves to dance
and to make the Church resound with songs
on the occasion of the deposition of God's Ark.
Behold: today heaven throws open its bosom
to receive her who brought forth the Great One;
the earth, receiving the source of life,
covered itself with blessings and beauty.
The angels make a choir with the Apostles
and watch over with reverence the Mother
of the King of life,
who passes from this life to the other.
Let us all kneel down before her and pray:
O Queen, do not forget those who are joined
to you by affinity and celebrate with faith
your holy dormition!

*Theophanus the "marked one"*

## Fertile earth of God
## from which has sprouted the ear of salvation

 lessed spouse of God, fertile earth
from which has sprouted without seed
the ear of salvation of the world,
make me worthy to eat it and to save myself.

O Most Holy Altar, bearer of the Bread of Life
who out of compassion descended from heaven
and bestowed on the world a new life,
make me worthy to taste it and to live.

Our Lady, welcome me with mercy
and give me your compassion;
keep me from blemish to receive
the precious pearl, and hallow me.

Mary, Mother of God, dwelling place
of the divine benevolence, through your prayers
make of me a chosen instrument
worthy of sharing
in the holy works of your Son.

O Holy Word of God, hallow all of me,
now that I prepare myself
for your holy mysteries,
through the prayers of your holy Mother.

O Pure One, full of divine grace,
you who brought forth Christ the Saviour,
I am about to draw near to the holy mystery:
I beg of you, purify me
from all blemish of body and soul!

On the point of receiving the Fire,
I shudder at being consumed like wax and grass.
Awesome mystery! How is it that I who am mire
am not destroyed
partaking of the Body and Blood of God?

God has taken substance from your immaculate Blood!
Thus the human race and the company of angels
sing glory to you, seeing with certainty
the Lord of the universe assume human form.

*Anonymous Prayer, 10th century*

# O Queen of the world
## hope and protection of the faithful

o not abandon me, O Lady most holy,
to the mercy of men;
receive the supplication of your servant;
I am oppressed by anguish
and it is hard for me to resist the pressure of evil.
Wretch that I am! I have no defence
nor do I know where to take refuge;
opposed from all sides
I find no other comfort but in you.
O Queen of the world, hope and protection
of the faithful, do not scorn my supplication
but obtain for me that which I need.

*Greek Votive Office*

# Do not send your servants back deluded

e who are oppressed by sin and misfortune
never cease to turn to the Mother of God;
contrite, we prostrate ourselves and
from the depth of our souls cry out:
Help us, O Queen, stir yourself to pity for us;
Hurry, we are about to succumb
under the weight of sin.
Do not send your servants back deluded,
for you alone are our hope!

O Mother of God, unworthy as we are,
we will never cease to make known your power.
If you had not been there to intercede for us,
who would have freed us from so many dangers?
Who would have kept us free till now?
O Queen, we will not turn away from you,
for you always save your servants
from all misfortune.

*Greek Votive Office*

# O merciful Mother of the God of love

ou, who gave birth to the source of immortality,
Most Holy Lady Mother of God,
light of the darkness of my soul,
O my hope and protection,
refuge, comfort and jubilation,
I thank you, for though unworthy,
you have made me a partaker of the immaculate body
and precious blood of your Son.

You who gave birth to the true light of the world,
enlighten the spiritual eyes of my heart.
You who gave birth to the source of immortality,
give life to me, dead through sin.

O merciful Mother of the God of love,
have pity on me and infuse in my heart
sorrow and repentance, humility in my thoughts,
and deliverance from the trials to which I am subjected.

Make me worthy, to my last breath,
to receive, without condemnation,
the sanctification that comes to me from your most pure
      mysteries
for the salvation of my soul and of my body.

Give me the tears of penitence and confession,
so that I can hymn my praise to you
and glorify you all the days of my life,
for you are blessed and glorified
for ever and ever. Amen.

*Anonymous Prayer, 10th century*

INDEX

# Sources

Below are some basic notes on the author of each hymn of praise, and the source of the original text.

*Page 12*

*The Magnificat* is a prophetic hymn springing from the heart of Mary on the day on which she visited her cousin Elizabeth. Together with the *Benedictus* of Zechariah (Luke 1:67-79) it became, quite early, part of the so-called *Canticles and Biblical Odes,* which, together with the Psalms, were used extensively in the early communities.
From the Grail translation.

*Page 14*

The *Sibylline Oracles* are 14 books of didactic poetry in Greek hexameters, dating from the 2nd century, which include Hebrew and Christian elements. Books 9 to 14 were discovered in 1817 by Cardinal Angelo Mai, paleographer and erudite humanist.
Translation from Syriac in J. Quasten, *Patrologia,* Turin, 1967, p. 147-148, adaptation of verses 6-10, Ode 19, by C. Berselli.

*Page 16*

The ancient prayer of *Sub tuum praesidium* is identified in this text, discovered in Egypt on a papyrus, probably dating from the 3rd century.
Greek text: *Horologion,* Rome 1937, p. 231-232.

*Page 18*

*St Hilary,* born in Poitiers, France, to an illustrious pagan family, was baptised late in life and, although already married, about 350 was elected bishop of his city. Stubborn opposition to Arianism made him unpopular with the Emperor Constantius who, in 356, banished him to Phrygia in Asia Minor. From there Hilary continued to defend Orthodoxy, and came into contact with Eastern theology and the study of doctrinal texts. Returning to Gaul, to his episcopal see, he continued his enlightened opposition to Arian heresy. His works reveal the depth of thought in which reason and faith unite. Some hymns, even if obscure and contorted, open the period of Latin hymnography. The text is taken from Migne, *Patrologia latina,* vol. 10, 66-67.

Page 20

This very short prayer, in which can be recognised the *Ave Maria*, was discovered in Egypt on an ostrakon (fragment of potsherd) which goes back to the 5th century.
Greek text: *Horologion*, ed. cit., p. 231-232.

Page 22

*Athanasius*, born in Alexandria in Egypt in 295, distinguished himself by defending the Catholic Faith against the Arians. At the Council of Nicaea in 325, which he had attended as secretary to Bishop Alexander, Athanasius commanded respect for his clarity of doctrine and strength of faith. In 328, on the death of Alexander, he was elected bishop of his native city, and remained so until his death in 373: a period of 45 years of toilsome and courageous episcopacy, in between persecution and various periods of exile as a result of the intrigues of the Arians. He left many works in defence of the faith in the divinity of Christ and of the divine Motherhood of Mary. The extract we quote is from a homily given on return from his second exile and preserved on a papyrus in the Museum of Ancient Egypt in Turin.
Text published in L.th.Lefort, *L'Homilie de st. Athenase des Papyrus de Turin*, in Le Muséon 71 (1958).

Page 24

*Gregory of Nyssa*, younger brother of Basil the Great, born in Caesarea of Cappadocia (now Kaisarieh in Turkey) about 335. Gifted with acute intelligence and encyclopaedic scholarship, Gregory was, however, lacking in practical perception. This makes clear the difficulty that he had in administering the diocese of Nyssa, of which he was elected bishop. Philosopher and theologian, he was acclaimed "pillar of truth" at the second Ecumenical Council in Constantinople in 381. He died in 395.
The hymn which is quoted here, came at the end of a homily on the Annunciation. Greek text: Migne, *Patrologia greca*, vol. 62, 765-766.

Page 28

*Ephraem Syrus* is the greatest of the Fathers of the Church in the Syrian tongue. Preacher, poet, exegete and controversial writer, he came to be called the "lyre of the Holy Spirit". Born in Nisibis (now Nisaybin in S.E. Turkey) about 306, he was ordained deacon in 337 and remained so until his death in 373. He left an enormous amount of literary works; his poems in the liturgical books of the Syrian Church are famous.
The hymn we present has come down to us in Greek. Greek text: *Byzantinische Zeitschrift* 19 (1909), p. 360.

*The Scroll of Ravenna,* discovered in 1833 in the Archives of Prince Anthony Pius of Savoy by scholars A. Ceriani and G. Porro of Turin, is a tattered parchment which measures 3.60 metres in length and 19 cm. in width. Written on both sides, the obverse contains Latin liturgical prayers, while on the reverse side are two letters exchanged between a Bishop of Ravenna and Sergius, Pope between 900 and 910. The scroll comes from the Ravenna Church and contains 40 prayers, thought by some to have been used in the main Canonical Hours of Advent. The prayer formulae, which probably originated at different times, and dictated by different authors, go back, according to the most informed critical sources, to the Churches of the Padana area, in a chronological span from the end of the 4th to the beginning of the 5th century.

Latin text: *Sacramentarium Veronense,* edited by L. C. Mohlberg, Rome 1956, Prayer n. 1365.

Scroll of Ravenna, Latin text: *Sacramentarium Veronense,* ed. cit., Prayer n. 1369.

The *Gallican Liturgy* was in use until the 9th century in the Latin West. The rite, in general, was more solemn and complete than the old Roman liturgy because of the wealth of its outward appearance and for the style of the prayers.

We quote here the text of the Preface of the Gallican Liturgy, drawn from the *Ordo antiquus gallicanus,* edited by Klaus Gamber, Regensburg 1965.

*Jerome* was born in Stridone in Dalmatia about 347; as a youth he went to Rome for classical studies. Irascible and restless by nature, his life was eventful and shaken by controversy. Jerome is known, above all, as the scriptural scholar who translated the Bible into Latin from the original Hebrew and Greek (the *Vulgate* Version) and also for his numerous commentaries. His Marian doctrine is outlined in some apologetic works and in various sermons and comments.

The text of Jerome's hymn to Our Lady is taken from *Treatise on Psalm 66, Corpus Christianorum Ecclesiasticorum Latinorum* (CSEL) vol. 78, p. 37-38.

The *Akathistos Hymn*, composed between the 5th and 6th centuries, is so-called because it was sung "standing", which is the meaning of the Greek word. It is, without doubt, the most famous hymn to Our Lady in the Byzantine Church; as popular among the Christians of the East as the Rosary is in the West. It is a masterpiece of theology, highest expression of contemplation and praise to the Virgin Mary. The hymn consists of 24 strophes or stanzas, corresponding to the letters of the Greek alphabet.

We give extracts from strophes 13-20, in the translation of C. Del Grande, Florence, Fussi 1948. Greek text is in *Horologion* ed. cit., 899-900.

These *Anonymous Hymns* (dating between the 5th and 6th centuries) are from the Book of Hours of the Greek Church. Here we find once again the Marian themes of preceding centuries, but in a more moderate and concise form, where the hymns end in a cry for help and supplication.

Greek text is in *Horologion,* ed. cit., p. 39.

Greek text is in *Horologion,* ed. cit., p. 138.

Greek text is in *Horologion*, ed. cit., p. 171. Prayer of the Sixth Hour.

Greek text is in *Horologion*, ed. cit., p. 173. Prayer of the Sixth Hour.

*Theodore*, Bishop of Ancyra of Galatia (now Ankara, capital of Turkey) lived in the first half of the 5th century, and was one of the most convinced defenders of the divine Motherhood of Mary. Six homilies attributed to him in which Mary occupies a position of affectionate regard, have come down to us.

We select an excerpt from the 4th homily. Greek text: Migne, *Patrologia greca*, vol. 77, 1393.

*Augustine* (354-430) born in Tagaste (now Souk-Ahras in Algeria). Converted at the age of 30, after a long cultural and spiritual struggle which is testified to in his *Confessions*, he was baptised by St Ambrose. Augustine, who became priest and bishop of the city of Hippo (now Bona), is and remains the powerful mind that brought together the values of the civilisation of his time, of which he was a skilled judge. Philosopher and theologian, a scholar of the most profound themes of the Faith and the defender of Orthodoxy against various heretical attacks, he was above all a pastor, conscious of the ministry of the word (he bequeathed more than 800 sermons). His literary activity was the most notable of all Roman antiquity.

We offer an extract from sermon 291, quoted by F. Spedalieri in *Maria nella scrittura e nella tradizione della Chiesa primitiva*, Messina, 1961; revised and abbreviated by C. Berselli. Latin text: Migne, *Patrologia latina*, vol. 38, 1319.

*Sedulius,* probably born in Italy in the 5th century (date uncertain), had spent part of his life in Greece. He was a priest, and probably a bishop. He was, with Prudentius, one of the most read and the most imitated of all the poets of the 5th century. He left five books, entitled *Paschale Carmen* (Easter Poem), which give an epic rendering of the history of salvation, from the Old Testament to the death and resurrection of Christ. His lyrical form is sincere, his creative form remarkable.

*Easter Poem* book 2, verses 48-53; 63-69. Latin text is in *Corpus Scriptorum Ecclesiasticorum Latinorum* (CSEL) vol. 10, p. 47-49.

*Ambrosian hymn.* Evidence going back to the earliest times testifies to the first Christians' custom of accompanying their sacred meetings with the singing of hymns. Extracts from the lyrical passages found in the Scriptures, especially in the psalms, were used as the text for these hymns, but little by little, original compositions appeared. St Ambrose, Bishop of Milan, is looked upon as the true inventor of sacred hymnology in the West, having introduced into the liturgy the singing of hymns which he composed. Following him, there was a flourishing of hymns which, alike in scale and structure, were generically termed "Ambrosian". It is not, therefore, an easy task to identify the writings of Ambrose in these chants. St Augustine gave evidence of the authenticity of four of the fifteen hymns as certainly being those of Ambrose. Among these there is the *Intende qui regis Israel,* for the feast of Christmas. In it emerges, delicately praised, the Mother of God.

Latin text is in *Innologia ambrosiana*, critical edition edited by Manlio Simonetti, Alba 1956.

*Peter Chrysologus* (Greek "golden-worded") native of Imola, was elected Bishop of Ravenna about 425 under Valentinianus II and Galla Placidia. From his numerous sermons we can draw outstanding elements of Christian life in Ravenna at the beginning of the 5th century. In his sermons, dealing for the most part with the mystery of the Incarnation, he frequently recalls the Mother of God.
The hymn quoted here is part of sermon 142 on the Annunciation of the Blessed Virgin Mary, quoted in F. Spedalieri, op. cit., p. 411, revised by C. Berselli. Latin text: Migne, *Patrologia latina*, vol. 52, 581 A.

*Eleutherius* (456-531 c.) was probably the first Bishop of Tournai in Flanders, in a troubled era, with the political horizon obscured following the downfall of Roman power and the invasion of the Franks. Neither the numerous anecdotes related in the story of his life, nor all the works attributed to him are supported by textual critics. His body is preserved in a beautiful sarcophagus in Tournai Cathedral.
We give an extract from his sermon on the Feast of the Annunciation. Latin text: Migne, *Patrologia latina*, vol. 65, 98-99.

*Modestus,* patriarch of Jerusalem, rebuilt the holy places destroyed by the Persians. He died in 634 and is honoured as saint in the Greek Church.
The hymn which appears here is included in an important discourse on the Annunciation which is attributed to him. Greek text: Migne, *Patrologia greca,* vol. 86, 3301-3305.

*Sophronius,* born in Damascus in Syria in 550. After having travelled widely in the East and to Rome with his friend Moschus, a monk and writer, he was elected Patriarch of Jerusalem in 634. When the Arabs of Caliph Omar, in 635-636, besieged and conquered the holy city, Sophronius undertook patient negotiations to extenuate the grievous consequences of the Arab invasion. He died in 638.
The hymn quoted here comes from a sermon on the Annunciation. Greek text: Migne, *Patrologia greca,* vol. 87, 3237, XVIII.

*Visigothic Book of Prayer* included in the treasured codex LXXXIX of the capitular library of Verona, is without doubt, the oldest text of the Mozarabic Liturgy. It was used in Spain before the Arab invasion, an epoch to which, undoubtedly, the manuscript has to be attributed. It is assumed, on established grounds, that it originated in the Church of Tarragona before 711. A text venerated for its antiquity and valid for the extraordinary richness of its prayer formulae (it contains 1211 complete prayers) it is of great importance for its biblical, liturgical, theological and hagiographical content and for its literary form.

Latin text is in *Oracional visigotica,* critical edition by D. José Vives, Barcelona 1946. Hymn on p. 64 is prayer 209; hymn on p. 66 is an extract from prayer 217; hymn on p. 68 is prayer 222; hymn on p. 70 is an excerpt from prayer 233.

*Page 72*

*Ildefonsus* of Toledo (617-667) bishop and writer, is known as the theologian of the Mother of God for his principal work on the Virginity of Mary, which is at the root of all the Marian literature in Spain. He wrote several works of a remarkable theological degree in which the traditional patrimony of the great Fathers is evoked. His mystical and legendary figure inspired the painter, El Greco, again and again, as well as being the subject of a comedy by Lope de Vega called *The Virgin's Chaplain.*

The hymn is taken from *Libellus de Corona Virginis,* chap. IX, Migne, *Patrologia latina,* vol. 96.

*Page 74*

*Germanus* (Constantinople 635-733) is a likeable saintly figure of a bishop caught up in the iconoclasm of Emperor Leo the Isaurian, to whose irrational fury he was opposed. Despite his being 96 years old he was, pointlessly, banished to exile. He left seven homilies on Our Lady. The emphasis he uses to entreat the Virgin was to be echoed in the writings of Bernard of Clairvaux.

*The homily on the Presentation* from which is reproduced the hymn on p. 74 is to be found in Migne, *Patrologia greca,* vol. 98, 292-309.

*Page 76*

*Andrew of Crete* (Damascus c. 660-Mitilene 740) was a monk, orator and hymnwriter. Elected Archbishop of Gortina in Crete, he took part in the conflict against monothelitism and in the defence of the cult of icons. He was a great writer of hymns, which to this day are preserved in the liturgical books of the Byzantine Church. He is said to be the inventor of a series of canons, long poetic compositions, divided into nine odes, each of which contains a certain number of strophes.

We give the IX Ode of Canon I of the Immaculate Conception of 8th December. Greek text: *Minea* (or Book of the Months), Rome 1888-1901, vol. 2, p. 439.

*John* of Damascus in Syria, was born about 675 into a family which was first in the service of the Byzantines and later of the Arabs. He succeeded his father in the office of governor of his native city. About 718 he embraced the monastic life and then later became a priest, dedicating himself immediately to preaching and the documentation of his works. He died in 749, leaving an abundance of theological, ascetic and liturgical works. His hymns to the Mother of God are to this day the patrimony of the Byzantine liturgical books. The Greek text of the hymn quoted here is in *Pentecostarion,* Rome 1883 p. 453.

The *Ethiopic Anaphora* (anaphora means canon) which we quote, is devoted entirely to Our Lady and goes back to the 8th century. Its title is *Anaphora in honour of Mary.*
An Italian translation is in G. Giamberardini, *Il culto mariano in Egitto,* vol. 2, Jerusalem 1974, p. 118.

*Joseph the Studite,* born in 726, followed his brother Theodore into the monastic life and in 807 became Metropolitan of Thessalonica. He died in 832, in exile. The Greek Church numbers him among her saints. He bequeathed a great number of homilies and hymns, many of them honouring Our Lady.
The Greek text of the hymn quoted is to be found in E. Follieri, *Un Theotokarian mariano del sec. XIV* (Cod. Mariano cl. 1, 6), Edizioni di Storia e Letteratura, Estratto dall'Archivio Italiano per la Storia della Pietà, vol. III, Rome 1961, p. 75-76. From Ode IX of the Canon for Friday.

*Peter of Argus* born in Constantinople at the end of the 9th century, became a monk and then Bishop of Argus in Peloponnisos. He was famous for his great works of charity for the poor. He left several sermons on Our Lady.
The hymn quoted here comes at the conclusion of a homily on the Presentation. Greek text: critically revised and Italian translation by E. Toniolo in *Marianum* 33 (1971) p. 18-47.

*Fulbert,* head of the Gallican Church and writer, was Bishop of Chartres from 1007. Reports on his pastoral activities are fragmentary. He rebuilt the Cathedral of Notre Dame in Chartres which had been

destroyed by fire. He was a great defender of the rights of the Church against the arrogance of the nobility, and was an austere spiritual director. In one of his sermons, the 9th, on the Sunday of the Annunciation, is found, probably confirming the popular piety of the times, the Invocation to Our Lady which we have chosen.
Text: Migne, *Patrologia latina,* 141, 358-359.

Page 88

*Hail, Star of the Sea* is the most popular hymn to Our Lady. It is full of tenderness and images, consistent with the sentiments and affection felt for Mary, which came to be invoked as a point of orientation on the difficult sea of life. The hymn has been attributed to Venanzio Fortunato (†601), to King Robert (†1031), to St Bernard (†1153). It dates, however, from before 1000, because it already appears in manuscript n. 95, preserved in the Swiss Monastery of St Gallen.

Pages 90-91

*Theophanus* with his brother Theodore was a monk in the "Lavra" in St Saba. He defended the cult of icons against the iconoclastic Emperors. For this he was sent to prison and exiled, together with his brother. When the persecution ceased, he became Metropolitan of Nicaea, where he died in the year 845. He was nicknamed "the marked one" or "the written-on" for having had words of derision for his defence of the cult of icons cut into his forehead with a red-hot iron. The two eulogies are taken from his hymnal compositions. Greek text: *Minea,* ed. cit., vol. 4, p. 183 from the Divine Office of Matins of 25th March (Hymn on p. 90 in this book); p. 409 from Vespers of 15th August (Hymn on p. 91 in this book).

Page 92

*Anonymous Prayer* (10th century). Greek text is in *Horologion,* ed. cit., p. 935. The Theotokia, or strophes dedicated to the Mother of God, are from the canon in preparation for Communion.

Pages 94-95

*Greek Votive Office.* The Greek Church, as a preparation for the Feast of the Assumption, is accustomed to sing each day, from the 1st to the 15th August, a Divine Office to Our Lady, called *paraklesis* or supplication. These two extracts are taken from this supplication. Greek text is in *Horologion* p. 911.

Page 96

*Anonymous Prayer* (10th century). Greek text is in *Horologion,* ed. cit., p. 966.

# INDEX OF HEADINGS

Printed in Italy by Istituto Grafico Bertello - 1981